"For Single People
Who Still Understand
the Value of Relationships"

Rob Hill S

Copyright Page

Spirit Filled Creations
3509 Kids Court
Chesapeake, Virginia 23323-1262

Copyright © 2012 by Rob Hill

Cover design by Donnie Ramsey

For information or to book an event contact publisher via email
SpiritFilledCreations7@gmail.com

Manufactured in the United States

ISBN 978-0-9653696-7-1 (paperback)

From Rob

I dedicate this book to my incredible parents, Frank and Monique Anderson. It is because of their unconditional love and example that I understand what a complete and healthy relationship is. Their passion, commitment, and fire for each other are the reason I can confidently refer to myself as a "hopeful" romantic.

I also dedicate this book to all the romantics who feel "hopeless." Great love is possible and healthy relationships are real. Not everything happens how we imagine it, but everything happens for a reason and it all happens the exact way that it's supposed to.

Lastly, I dedicate this book to every reader, supporter, and client who has ever trusted me with the issues of their heart. Your faith in me has been a constant reminder of God's plan for me. Love, is truly a life changer.

Table of Contents

Chapter One

Common Misconceptions of Relationships

A relationship is what you make it. It's not a trap, it's not a prison, and it's not something you get into just to pass time. A healthy relationship is a support system for the storms and some good company in the midst of the chaos. There are no perfect relationships, because there are no perfect people, but a good healthy relationship is a priceless possession.

For Single People Who Still Understand the Value of Relationships

A Relationship Is A 100/100 Partnership

It's not 70/30, not 60/40, not even 50/50. A true relationship is 100% them and 100% you. You cannot give half of yourself and expect to get all of your partner. It just doesn't work that way. If both of you are not fully invested in the relationship, it will not grow. An unbalanced relationship is a dying relationship. Love can't flourish if it isn't given the effort it requires to grow. Don't play games to get more out of your relationship. If you can't be true to yourself and get results then things need to change. Healthy relationships require effort and if you and your partner aren't 100% committed to the others happiness, then you're wasting each other's time.

100% them and 100% you.

A Relationship Is Supposed To Be An Outlet

Your relationship should be your place of refuge. When the world gets rough, your relationship should be what comforts you. Your relationship should be what you lean on for stability when life is pushing you in different directions. It should be the place where you can unapologetically be yourself. You shouldn't have to hide your frustrations or put on a mask to make it seem like everything is okay. You have to be dedicated to being there for your partner in a way that makes them feel confident in coming to you in their time of need. If they're sad, it is on you to be their sunshine. If they're angry, it is on you to be their peace of mind. A relationship that can handle the trials is built to celebrate many triumphs.

A Relationship Is A Compliment

A relationship can only be a compliment to you; it will never be something that completes you. Your relationship shouldn't be your world; it should be something that adds value to what's already in your world. A successful relationship with somebody else is the result of a successful relationship with yourself. A relationship should enhance what's already in you. If you have a vision for your life, the relationship you're in should enlarge that. Don't make the mistake of expecting a relationship to instantly become the solution to problems you ran away from when you were single. Secure happiness, peace, and comfort from yourself through a relationship with God and then seek chances to share it with someone else. Don't be so consumed with love that you forget your responsibilities to your life. You shouldn't lose all joy just because it didn't work out with somebody who once brought you happiness.

A successful relationship with somebody else is the result of a successful relationship with yourself

A Relationship Is A Friendship

A relationship is a friendship. It is a union of two people committed to being there for one another regardless of circumstance. As with any friendship, your relationship needs trust, communication, and honesty to bring you fulfillment. If you can't laugh and joke with your partner then you probably won't be able to communicate and agree with them when it's time to. Before you commit to a relationship with somebody, be certain that you have the

4

foundation of a strong friendship. If you're a communicator, get with somebody who does more than shut down when things don't go right. If you feed off emotion, get somebody who knows how to respect them in a way that doesn't make you feel overly sensitive. Most successful relationships are the result of successful friendships. That's because the best ingredient in a good friendships is understanding, so be with somebody that "gets you."

Be invested in your relationship physically, mentally, spiritually, and emotionally

A Relationship Is Supposed To Be Fun

Your relationship should stay new, exciting, and young for as long as you can keep it that way. Be open minded enough to keep things fresh and spontaneous. The best relationships are those that continue to find new ways to grow and evolve with one another. Don't get so caught up in a routine that your partner starts to get bored. Take every chance you can to do something different or experience something new. Nothing draws two people closer than connecting through new experiences, regardless of whether they're good or bad. Make sure your relationship is a collection of moments not a deathbed for routines. The worst thing you can do to a good relationship is allow things to get old and predictable.

A Relationship Is A Commitment To More Than Monogamy

Your relationship should be a commitment to dependability and trustworthiness. It should be committed to being loyal and understanding. Don't allow a fear of commitment to be the reason you never have anything consistent. Be invested in your relationship physically, mentally, spiritually, and emotionally. Your partner shouldn't have to be content just because you don't cheat physically, especially if you're not giving them what they need in the other areas. If you're unable to commit in your relationship entirely then be man or woman enough to let your partner choose whether or not they want to stay.

Take things step by step; don't be willing to act married but unwilling to actually get married.

A Relationship Is Not A Marriage

A boyfriend is a boyfriend and a girlfriend is a girlfriend. Period. If you ever get the roles confused, break both words down to their simplest form. Nowhere in them will you find husband or wife. Your relationship shouldn't be dictated by a "title" but there should be clear boundaries. Some things are better saved for matrimony. Don't get so caught up in emotions that you start giving away things that should be earned. Take things step by step; don't be willing to act married but unwilling to actually get married. If you have doubts, express the doubts and be committed to working through them. Don't get so comfortable in the relationship that you get stagnant. When the roles begin to blur a little bit, take a second to redefine your position in one another's life. The strongest relationships are those that can revisit agreements, revise situations, and remove whatever is unnecessary for the sake of continuing towards a healthy future.

If you want to find some sort of fulfillment, stop wasting time looking for cheap thrills and fun nights.

A Relationship Is Not Something To Be In Just So You Aren't Lonely

Don't play with another person's heart just because you're selfish with yours. If you can't be alone without feeling lonely then ultimately the relationship you build will be about as strong as a sand castle. You can't expect a relationship to complete you if you don't know what's missing in you. If you want to find some sort of fulfillment, stop wasting time looking for cheap thrills and fun nights. You can't be one foot in and one foot out when it comes to happiness and love. If you are scared of being lonely, it's because you're scared of what you're lacking. Don't waste somebody's time just because you are aimlessly passing time; that's what selfish people do. Let God do whatever it is required to complete you so HE can bring you a relationship designed to compliment you.

A Relationship Is Not A Public Playground

Everybody shouldn't have free access to your business or know what's going on in your relationship. I cannot stress this next statement enough. What goes on between you and your partner should stay between you and your partner. You may have times where you all aren't communicating but that isn't an opportunity to share every detail with anybody that'll listen. Keep your relationship secure. If you do not, every time you "vent" you'll be inviting more and more separators in to tear you both apart. If you can't talk about it, write each other letters. Find healthy ways to communicate with one another, other than silent cries for attention on social networks. The more people you share your relationship problems with, the less solutions you will find. Remember: the weakest relationships are the ones with more than two people in them.

You have to put in the work and you have to be willing to compromise if you want your relationship to survive the trying times.

A Relationship Is Not Something That Love Alone Can Maintain

A relationship needs much more than love to last. Happiness requires much more than deep sentiments and cute moments. If you are selfish, inconsiderate, and lack compassion then relationships are not for you. If you are against sacrifice and only look to protect yourself then a relationship is not for you. If you aren't willing to give genuinely and not feel used if things don't work out then a relationship is not for you. You have to put in the work and you have to be willing to compromise if you want your relationship to survive the trying times. It is not enough to get so used to saying "I love you" that you forget to take advantage of chances to show it. You have to invest much more than feelings into a relationship in order for it to grow. You have to put your time, effort, and faith all in, if you expect to get anything out.

For Single People Who Still Understand the Value of Relationships

Chapter Two

Qualities of Strong Relationships

A strong relationship is a treasure. To have somebody, through thick and thin, up and down, good and bad is a blessing. If you don't understand the qualities of strong relationships you'll be stuck dealing with the frustrations of weak ones. Ineffective communication is the number one cause of defective relationships.

For Single People Who Still Understand the Value of Relationships

Identity

Every relationship needs an identity. Make sure what you and your partner stand for as individual's compliments both of you as a couple. Your partner is a reflection of you so make sure that what they're showing represents you in the best way possible. The person you choose to love can and will have an impact on the life you live. Example: Barack Obama would not be "Barack" if Michelle was not "Michelle." You and your partner don't have to agree on everything, but you do need to share similar morals, values, and principles. When you agree at the core, it's easier to work things out on the surface.

...push your partner to grow in all aspects of life

Goal Oriented

Set goals that you and your partner can help the other to reach. If your relationship has healthy goals then it is a relationship with unlimited horizons. It is important to push your partner to grow in all aspects of life. Helping them become a better person will make them a better partner for you. A relationship with two people who cannot motivate each other is a relationship with an expiration date. You have to be able to look over at your partner and gain inspiration or feel propelled to do more. A part of what connects most strong relationships is the constant challenge, whether it's individual challenges or collective challenges. Care about your partner enough to help them reach new highs in every area of their life, be it professionally, spiritually, or physically. If they have a goal, a part of your commitment to the relationship requires you to help them reach it.

Understanding

Sometimes it's not always about agreeing; your relationship can really flourish from simply understanding and appreciating differences. Don't expect things to always be seen from your point of view because that can easily come off as selfishness. Real love is selfless; it's using everything in you to protect your lover's heart with the same passion that you guard yours with. When situations occur, be able to look at things from your partner's stance and understand where they may be coming from. Your relationship can gain strength from a willingness to look at things from multiple perspectives. You aren't always right and you won't always be wrong, but sometimes you have to care enough to find common ground.

If you present a problem, have a solution

Honesty

Do not use honesty as your excuse to complain excessively. Be honest, but be honest in a productive matter. If you present a problem, have a solution, and have one that brings peace to the situation not just a boost for your ego. Honesty is something used to bring resolve, it's supposed to help the situation. So, before you ask for it, make sure you're capable of handling the truth. Don't ask for honesty and then reject it just because it wasn't what you wanted to hear. Be honest with yourself, the worst lies in love are the ones we tell ourselves. Learn how to use honesty in ways that release you from the power of your mistakes. Allow truth and honesty to align you and your partner on the same path. Lies only create divides in relationships.

Respect

Understand what boundaries not to cross in your relationship. Don't constantly throw your partner's mistakes out there, especially if it's something you've claimed to have moved on from. Respect boundaries and operate out of love, not out of spite. Don't be so focused on making a point, that you lose your love. It doesn't matter how angry, sad, or frustrated you are, don't ever let your pride cause you to be petty. Treat your partner with the same level of respect you want to be treated with. Don't attack them every time they fall short of your expectations. Don't ridicule them every time they make a bad decision. Love isn't a competition; it's a dedication. Respect your partner enough to forgive them and let it go. Respect them enough to communicate effectively, not to demean them. Healthy relationships always maintain a fair level of respect.

Respect and Accountability go hand in hand

Accountability

Playing the blame game is the fastest way to play yourself and lead you towards a lonely life. If finding solutions is more important than finding faults in your relationships then you have something strong. Don't get so caught up in wrong and right that you never get past pointing fingers. Learn how to say, "I messed up but I'm going to do better," and actually mean it. Accountability is huge because it shows you accept where you fall short and that you care enough to improve. If you care about the situation enough to be angry, then be real enough with yourself to put forth effort towards making it better

God

Strong relationships encourage one another spiritually. Your love for your partner can be enhanced through your love for God. Faith connects people and having common hopes will draw real lovers closer. Don't be afraid to reach new levels spiritually with your partner; prayer strengthens good relationships destined by God. God is the glue that helps you hold on when pride tells you to quit. If the only level you and your partner connect on is physical then there won't be much to hold together when your youth fades. Make sure you're building something with somebody who wants to pray with you more than they want to play with you.

...do right ...even when things are going wrong.

Faith

If you don't have faith in them then you don't need to be with them. If you don't believe in your partner it will be impossible for the both of you to share a productive future together. It's important to know that without a doubt, no matter what happens, the person you care about isn't moving with ill intentions. Have faith that they respect and cherish you enough to do right by you even when things are going wrong. If you don't believe you can trust anybody, your thoughts won't allow you to find anybody trustworthy. Have faith in your judgment of character and realize that just because you were hurt before does not mean everybody wants to hurt you now. Have enough faith to believe that some people are still true. Not everyone comes with plans to bring you regrets and pain, but if that's all you think about, then that's all you'll know.

16

Priorities

Make sure what's important in your relationship stays important and doesn't get put on the back burner. There will always be work, there will always be things to do, but you won't always have time to appreciate each other. If you're in a relationship that you want to last then you must make that person's smile and happiness a priority in your life. Don't get so caught up in what everybody else is doing but be completely focused on making what you have the best it can possibly be. If bringing your partner joy isn't a priority to you then the relationship isn't important to you. Situations begin to turn sour when priorities are out of order.

Excitement is what will draw you

Spontaneity

Never grow tired of looking for new ways to keep things fresh in your relationship. Excitement is the driving force that will draw you and your partner closer. Continuously giving your lover something to look forward to is a great way to keep your relationship strong. Regardless of work or how demanding your schedule is, you should always keep things interesting. Don't use being consistent as an excuse to be boring. There is always something new to do when you're open-minded. If you truly care, it doesn't matter how much you have going on because you will find a way to make your partner feel special. Whether it is a random text messages, love notes, or simple gifts, keep the spontaneity going.

For Single People Who Still Understand the Value of Relationships

Chapter Three

What Today's Women Should Know About Today's Men

There are key things women need to understand about men when it comes to finding, sustaining, and enjoying a valuable relationship. The most important is all men have similarities but all men are not the same. If you can understand a man without feeling the need to judge him then it will be easier to keep him. Men want a woman who cares enough to enhance him but appreciates him enough not to want to change him.

For Single People Who Still Understand the Value of Relationships

Men Want A Relationship

A good man, a real man, an honest man, genuinely wants a relationship. Men just don't want the stress, arguments, and issues that they've experienced in previous relationships in the one that they have with you. It's not on you to prove to him that you're different than the women that came before you; all you have to do is be yourself. Men desire companionship and consistency just as women do; they're just not inclined to rush into having it. Men operate on a different time clock than women, so it's important for you to understand that when he's ready for a relationship it will be clear. You cannot force a man to be ready for what you have to offer and you shouldn't have to. If the man is smart, he'll recognize that you're a good woman and understand that you would be a valuable part of his pursuit of true success.

Men desire companionship and consistency just as women do; they're just not inclined to rush into having it.

Men Need Support

Build your man up with positive actions and encouraging words. Make sure he knows that you really believe in him. If you invest in his dreams now, he won't rest until the fruits of that hard work bring you happiness later. Men appreciate women who understand the importance of being supportive. Don't ever pass up an opportunity to be there for him. It doesn't matter how small the event is; knowing you took the time to make it, matters to him. If he's not doing anything for you to support then it's your chance to tap into his potential and get him moving. Supporting a good man is a balance of celebrating him while challenging him. Be the greatest fan of his life and he'll make sure you're a superstar in his.

Men Like Challenges

Ladies, if he doesn't have to work to get you then he won't work to keep you. Be intriguing enough to make him want to know more about you. The honest truth is that if you can't make a man wonder then more than likely you won't be able to make him commit either. Don't give him everything he wants on his time; give it to him when you're ready for him to have it. Men are patient when it comes to quality, so if he feels like you're worth it, he'll face whatever challenge you present him with. However, to be a challenge to him does not mean for you to play games with him. The minute he feels like you're playing, he'll stop trying. Make him work for your time, make him work for your attention, and make him work for your feelings. If you give it to him easily he'll leave it easily. Challenge him; if he doesn't rise up to it then he's below your standards.

If he's not doing anything for you to support then it's your chance to tap into his potential and get him moving.

Men Desire A Companion

Be a friend and a partner to your man before anything else. Listen to him and agree with him when you can. And most importantly, try your hardest to see where he's coming from. Don't try to be his mother. No man wants to be scolded like a child by the woman he loves, regardless of whether or not he's acting like one. He'll forget things and make mistakes, but it's important for you to understand that nagging him will never be an effective way to get his attention. Let him know you're there for him and not against him. Care enough to talk to him in a way that lets him know you're still on his side. Be there, right beside him, not in front of him, not behind him, and not standing over him. Make him feel like you're in his corner and not the one he's fighting.

Men Like Confidence

Make sure you know the true value of what you bring to the table and be confident in your womanhood. Men are attracted to women who know their value; they just don't like women who try to show their worth by ignoring his. Be confident and sure of yourself. The only time a man will have a problem is when you come off as full of yourself. It's great that you have your own but don't forget to make him feel like he can still contribute in some way to your life. You don't have to play smaller than you are, however, don't make him feel less than while you're building yourself up. If he's a real man, your confidence in yourself will make him feel like you're an asset to his life. Your ability to tell AND show him that you can and will make him a better all-around man will make you desirable.

Be confident and sure of yourself.

Men Need Their Ego Stroked

You don't have to lie to him, but a wise woman understands that if she makes him feel strong like Superman, he'll treat her like Wonder Woman. Even the most confident man needs the occasional reassurance. It doesn't matter how many awards, honors, or titles he holds, men love it when their woman build them up. When he stumbles and hesitates, remind him of who he is to you and the greatness you see in him. He may not be the prince charming from the fairytales but he can be the King of your dreams. Simple words like "you can do it" or "I believe in you" can get even the most stagnant man moving when encouraging words come from a genuine woman. If you know he's a good man, take the time to say the little things needed to make him feel like one.

If you really want him to remember then you will have to put your pride and emotions to the side and take the time to remind him

Men Need Reminders

Everyone forgets. It is a flaw of our humanity. And men, well, men forget a little more than normal; so it's important to give him occasional reminders. It's not that he forgets because he doesn't care, it's just that you, as with most women, naturally pay attention to details better than men. If you really want him to remember then you will have to put your pride and emotions to the side and take the time to remind him. If you're not willing to remind him, then it is not fair for you to have an attitude when and if he forgets. If you're the type of woman who keeps track of three-month anniversaries and what you all did on your third date then you can't realistically expect him to remember all of that. It doesn't mean he cares any less about the relationship; it just means that other things stick out to him. Remind him when you want him to remember. It won't kill you to do so. If he's a quick learner then he won't need you to give him more than one or two reminders.

24

Men Desire A Fair Balance

If he feels like nothing he does will make you happy then he will stop trying. Be mindful of how you treat him and the way you talk to him. Just because you're angry with him doesn't mean you have to start a war with him. Learn how to show him you're unhappy without coming off as if you take pride in how well you can get mad. If nothing he does can make it right at the moment, be woman enough to tell him that you need additional time to get over it. Keep it consistent. If he makes you mad, communicate the offense so that in the future he can learn from it. Don't just get mad with him for the sake of being mad. Nothing frustrates a man more than dealing with an attitude he doesn't know what he did to cause. Keep a fair balance. He shouldn't feel like he's dating two different women every time it's "that time of the month" for you

Learn how to show him you're unhappy without coming off as if you take pride in how well you can get mad

Men Love Having Something To Wonder About

If he feels he knows everything there is to know about you, then his interest in you slowly starts to die. This doesn't mean you should hide parts of you from him, it just means you should continue to mature and develop personally. It's vital that you keep growing as a woman so that you'll always have "more" to show him. However, don't be so mysterious that he grows restless trying to figure you out. You must be balanced in your intentions. Make sure he feels like he knows you, but keep growing, so he feels the need to get to know you better. Do things to strike his imagination and get the wheels in his head turning. Be fascinating. Be so captivating that he can't stop thinking about you. Become what he daydreams about.

Men Like Surprises

It's important for you to know what he likes and what he's into. You can use that information to show him something about you that he probably doesn't know. Pay enough attention to him to be able to show him something he hasn't seen before. Be different, be refreshing, and be exciting. Men like woman who are fun and he'll want to spend more time with you if he knows he'll have a good time with you. Don't let sex be the only time you're fun to him. Read, do research, or ask random questions so that you're constantly keeping things new. Few things are more attractive to a real man than a woman who can teach him something.

Chapter Four

What Today's Men Should Know About Today's Women

A real woman would rather spend her time cherishing a good man versus wasting her time chastising a bad one. A good woman is easy to please but hard to impress. If your actions don't show her what she's looking for, then, your words will be ignored.

For Single People Who Still Understand the Value of Relationships

Real Women Look For a Partner, Not a Savior

As a man you should compliment her life; don't try to control it. Make her feel like you want her in your life by appreciating the woman she is. If you want her to "need" you because it makes you feel like more of a man, you'll only hold her back as a woman. A real woman wants a partner, not a savior. So if she's looking for you to do everything for her than more than likely she is not the one for you. If you're her man then she trusts that you're there for her and that's all she needs to know. Don't try to limit her just to save her stress; she's a real woman so she knows what she can handle. Be her partner, walk beside her and support her when she needs it. Invest into her dreams just as you would want her to invest in yours. A woman with a dream is the best partner to a man with a vision.

...give your word and keep it

Women Want A Strong Man

As a man you should be able to make a decision and stick by it. Don't waver back and forth because women respect and value certainty. Things change but you have to be able to adapt. Don't be the kind of man that breaks down when things don't go perfectly or as you planned. A man should be able to give his word and keep it. A man that can't keep his word is a man that can't keep a woman. She has to be able to trust you. If she feels like you don't value your own words enough to stand by them, she knows you won't value her heart. As a man you should be able to be consistent without being predictable. Know what to do, when to do it, and how to do it. If you make her feel like she has to teach you everything, she'll feel more like your mother than your woman.

Women Need You To Listen

You have to learn how to respond to her without having a ready rebuttal to what she's said. Hear her out and just because you don't agree that doesn't mean you need to voice it at that moment. You shouldn't try to make her feel crazy for what she's feeling and don't assume you know what she's going to say. One of the best qualities a strong man can have is to be a good listener. Sometimes, more than anything, women want to be heard and received in a way that doesn't make them feel like they're stupid for caring the way that they do. Even if you don't want to hear it at the time, it won't hurt you to listen. There may be more to what she's saying than what's on the surface, so don't miss it and lose your woman just because you didn't care to listen.

...don't assume you know what she's going to say

Women Desire Something Exclusive

Women enjoy knowing what they have in you is desired by most but not available to everyone. Don't make her feel like she's sharing you with the world and getting the short end of the stick. She's smart; she knows she can't have all of your time, so make sure that when she gets some, you're giving her quality attention. As a smart man, you have to understand the importance of "firsts." Do something with her to show her that she's set apart. You should never miss a chance to make your woman feel special. You don't have to get her name tattooed on your face, but make it clear that what you have with her, nobody else has. There's nothing like having your own and women appreciate that exclusive feeling like no other. Make sure that what you give her is specifically and especially for her, nobody else.

Women Only Trust Consistency

Don't tell her if you can't show her. And don't show her if you can't do it consistently. Any man can make the right move one time, but you have to be a real man to make the right moves consistently. You can't expect her to trust you if you haven't consistently given her reason to. A woman understands that with trust comes vulnerability. So, if she lets her guard down enough to trust you then make sure you care enough to protect her. Don't say you will, unless you will. Don't say you care if your actions are going to show that you don't. Your actions will dictate how much and to what degree you are trusted. What you say has to match what you do. Consistency earns trust and repeated inconsistencies earn doubt. Your actions will influence which she will choose.

She's smart; she knows she can't have all of your time, so make sure that when she gets some, you're giving her quality attention.

Women Are Intrigued By Mystery

You need to understand the difference between mystery and secrecy. Give her enough of you to make her want more, but don't do it in a way that makes her think you're hiding something. Make her wonder; don't make her worry. Be so rich with personality and substance that you're constantly keeping her intrigued. Make her feel like she gets to know more and more of you as the days go on. However, it's important not to fall into the secretive side. If she feels you're hiding something, her intuition will have her watching you versus enjoying her time with you. Be willing to show her your cards, but don't be predictable in how you play them.

Women Long To Be Assured

Men, let her know that she's the only one you want. It doesn't matter if you've known her two weeks or twenty years. Take random moments just to let her know that she's still special to you. Assurance doesn't require a lot of effort at all. However, it does require you to care enough to do a little more. If you don't feel like she's worth going the extra mile for then you shouldn't be with her. But if you know that she's worth it then take the time to give her everything you know she deserves. Write her a nice note and slip it in her purse. Show her that you're willing to do more than just what's expected of you. Make sure she knows you're not just used to her, but that you still appreciate her.

If you don't feel like she's worth going the extra mile for then you shouldn't be with her

Women Appreciate The Simple Things

You should never miss an opportunity to make her smile. The cliché is accurate when it said, actions speak louder than words. Do whatever you can, whenever you can to make sure she knows how valuable she is to you. Let her know that she's on your mind, and let her know often. She'll judge how much you care for her by the effort you put towards the simple things. On her bad days, it's the simple things that truly make a difference. She may never complain or make things a big deal, but making it a point to do something nice for her means more than you will ever know. It's not about being the perfect man and it's not about doing everything right. What it is is being willing to make it clear that you care enough to try.

Women Want Substance

You should care for her past her physicality. She'll know if you're in it for the wrong reasons, and if she senses that you're only in it for her looks, she'll look right past you. You should be able to connect with her emotionally, spiritually and socially, not just physically. Some women may be content with you only caring for their looks, but a real woman knows she has much more to offer. Don't let your money be the only thing you have to offer her. A woman wants a man that can boost her in all areas of her life, not just a man who can add clothes to her closet. Show her something different, show her something about you that sets you apart; don't just show her things.

Some women may be content with you only caring for their looks, but a real woman knows she has much more to offer

Women Need Honesty

If you can't keep it 100% with her then just keep it to yourself. There's no need to play games and give her the run around if you aren't planning on taking the relationship anywhere. Not only does a real woman need honesty, she respects it. She may not like everything you do or say, but she'll always be woman enough to respect you for being honest about it. The worst thing you can do as a man is make a good woman think trusting you was a mistake and a waste of time. Women are honest enough with themselves not to expect you to be a perfect man but they do expect you to be a real man. If she's important to you, care about her enough to be honest, upfront, and true. Let your actions match your words and be man enough to stand by your mistakes. If honesty is a problem for you then having a healthy successful relationship will be impossible for you.

For Single People Who Still Understand the Value of Relationships

Chapter Five

Mistakes Women Make in Dating

Be confident. Be passionate. Be intelligent. Nothing sets a woman further away from happiness than insecurities and unnecessary baggage. Understand who you are as a woman in a way that radiates to men that you are one of one, not one of many.

For Single People Who Still Understand the Value of Relationships

Pay Attention To Him

You have to learn to see more than what is on the surface. Real men show much more than they tell. If you're a smart woman, you won't bring up drama before you find out how his day was. Pay enough attention to him to know how he's feeling or at least know when he needs positive attention from you. Ask him how he's feeling, ask him what's on his mind, and ask what he thinks about certain things. Men are attracted to women who can talk about more things than their emotions. A real man doesn't care to share his life with the world, but he will care to let you in if you show him you truly care. Don't stalk his social networks and make them too big of a deal for if you do, he'll feel you're trying to control him. If all you pay attention to is what he does socially, then you're slipping, and it's probably why you feel left out emotionally.

...arguing is not the way to get it

Don't Make Yourself The Enemy

If all he's doing is arguing with you then you can bet he'll give you less and less of him. Be tactical in how you approach situations when you have a problem with him. By instinct, if he feels like you are attacking him he will get defensive. Be the kind of woman that can get her point across without making him feel like it's going to lead to an argument. For men, peace of mind is priceless, so whoever is causing the most headaches will get ignored the fastest. If you want more from him, arguing is not the way to get it. Don't make him feel like fighting with you is the only option when things go wrong. Communicate with him in a way that makes him want to receive what you're saying. If all you do is yell when you're frustrated, he may hear you but he won't be listening.

Maintain A Degree Of Discretion

Men do not care what your friends think about the problems you two may have. Communicate with him before you talk about him. If your friends are the only people you go to when you want to vent, then you're cheating your man of the chance to genuinely be your man. He may be the reason for the problem, but give him a fair chance to become the solution. Be mindful of the things that you share because even though you may forgive him, people won't forget what you told them. No man is fond of dealing with the attitudes of more women than he has to when it comes to his relationship. Don't tell his business to other people. Men don't mind you sharing things like your frustrations with work and etcetera. However, the real problems arise when you share things about him and your relationship that he feels other people just don't need to know.

A scar is the evidence of a healed wound.

Don't Give Him The Hell The Last Man Brought To You

If you haven't done the required work to be healed from the wounds of your past relationships then you have no business starting a new one. Love is a battlefield and we all get scarred but the profound thing about a scar is that it's the evidence of a healed wound. It's a sign that even though you carry the memory of the hurt, you no longer have the pain. But when you move on too soon and fail to heal properly, you only make the wounds deeper and harder to heal. Moving on to the next won't help you get over the past. It will only give you more reasons to avoid issues you need to work on and fix in the future. When you

38

carry baggage from situation to situation all you do is add unnecessary strain to a situation that doesn't deserve it. Just because the last man was a bad man, doesn't mean every man after him will be the same.

Don't Assume He Understands

Make whatever you're trying to say crystal clear. If you choose not to then you can't get an attitude when he interprets things another way. You may feel like you shouldn't have to say certain things but if you want to be understood, be wise enough to communicate effectively. It doesn't hurt you to explain yourself a little further just for the sake of avoiding the possibility of a future argument. When you make things clear you don't allow any room for confusion. Assumptions only succeed when communication fails. There are some smart men out there but none of them are capable of reading minds. If you want to be understood then you must present your case in a way he can understand. This process will eliminate his excuses at the end of the day. Don't let assumptions bring you unnecessary frustrations. If you make it plain, then you also make it easy on yourself.

Assumptions only succeed when communication fails

Don't Focus Too Much On His Past

Let's be honest and realistic and admit that what happened before you does not concern you. The bigger you make the things that happened in his past, the smaller he'll make your role in his future. Right now is what you. Don't spend it worrying about the things and people before you. It's an exercise in futility, especially since you can't change any of it. He probably made some mistakes before you and he'll probably make some while dealing with you, but he's human. If you don't think he's worth looking past his mistakes then he's not a man you need to be dating. Don't force yourself to deal with certain things because people say you should. If it's something you just can't get over, then you have to do what's best for you. Just don't bring up his past every chance given, especially if you say you're over it.

He will appreciate you more if you receive him when he tries to open up and don't force him to talk when he's not ready to.

Be Careful Not To Overstep Boundaries

Don't make him regret the fact that he let you in. When he opens up to you, don't shoot him down or act like he's being over sensitive. No man wants his woman to make him feel soft. So if he's trying to let you in, just take it for what it is. He will appreciate you more if you receive him when he tries to open up and don't force him to talk when he's not ready to. Be patient with him and know that when it's time to come around, he will. Don't let your efforts to "support" him come off as you judging him. Understand when you should speak up and when it's better to just be there for him.

Appreciate Him As An Individual

You should enhance who he already is and don't try to change him into somebody else. If you feel like you have to change him, then you're subconsciously admitting that you know he isn't the man for you. It may be hard for you to accept that the man you want isn't the man you need or the man you want him to be, but you can't change him. You have to take him for who he is and accept him for who he is not. Some people change, some people grow and mature, and some people just stay the exact same; all you can do is accept that. If he has potential and he's showing you that he wants to be better, then find out where he wants to go and help him get there. But if you're making what you want clear and he's not living up to that, don't play games trying to change him into what you want him to be. A man is going to be himself. He is not going to change until he's ready or sees a need for change. As a woman, you have to be prepared to accept the fact that every man won't be who you think he needs to be. The one for you will be prepared for you and you won't need to change him in order for you to be happy.

Understand who you are and who you aren't

Don't Move In Spite

When you make a man think your intent is to hurt him then his instincts will cause him to run from you. Regardless of how angry he makes you or how frustrated you may get, move with genuine intentions, not out of spite. You can't get anywhere with him if you're not being genuine with him. If you're trying to teach him a lesson out of spite, the only thing he'll learn is new ways to resent you. Playing get back will only get you left behind. If you

41

want him to do certain things a different way then you will have to communicate and let him know. If he did something to hurt your feelings, you must let him know. Playing games accomplishes on thing...getting you played.

If you've been playing a side role just to keep him then don't get mad when he doesn't consider you when he's looking for a leading lady

Define Your Role For Yourself And Be True To It

Don't look for him to give you a "position," because if you do so, he will put you where it is convenient for him but completely wrong for you. Understand who you are and who you are not. If you've been playing a side role just to keep him then don't get mad when he doesn't consider you when he's looking for a leading lady. If you're a wise woman, you will always put yourself in the right position. Please don't wait around aimlessly for a man to tell you, your worth. If he doesn't see that you're valuable then it's his lost. But you cannot wait around trying to prove to him how great you are. If you're a good catch, then be a good catch regardless of who has their hands out to catch you. Be true to who you know you are and the right man will recognize that.

Chapter Six

Mistakes Men Make In Dating

Be understanding. Be attentive. Be trustworthy. A wise man doesn't have to be the smoothest or the best looking. He just has to be smart enough to listen. Men that understand the importance of the simple things will always be desirable to good women.

For Single People Who Still Understand the Value of Relationships

Don't Be Too Quick To Try And Solve The Problem

Address and empathize with your woman on the issue at hand and make sure she knows you understand the reason for it. Then, with her permission, try to move forward towards solving the problem. You may feel like it's pointless but sometimes you have to put what you think about it aside and respect how she feels about it first. Some women believe understanding is the key to problem solving. Show your woman that you care to understand and that you're man enough to fix whatever is wrong. For some women, sympathizing with them is more important than finding the solution to their problem. Understand her in a way that doesn't make her feel like you're analyzing her. She may not have a reason that she can tell you for everything she feels, but sometimes you just have to be her man and tell her "I'm here and I'm willing to help in whatever capacity."

Show your woman that you care to understand and that you're man enough to fix whatever is wrong.

Compliment Her

Of all the times your woman is complimented, none mean more than when they come from you, the man she cares about. It doesn't matter whether she gets it a million times or a billion times, when you have her heart, you're the only one that matters. If you're a smart man, you'll never miss the chance to make your woman feel beautiful. Whether it's complimenting her hair, noticing her eyebrows, or telling her you love her smile, make sure you compliment her. Let her know that you're paying attention to her and that you like what you see. Let her know that you've noticed the new changes and that she looks even better than before. The smallest of compliments from you can truly make her day

45

Don't Get Comfortable Too Fast

If you start off a certain way and maintain a standard then don't fall off just because you think you have her. A real man never stops putting in the work needed to keep his woman. A real man understands that what he puts into a good woman will always come back in her efforts to make him a great man. As the relationship grows things naturally change but how you make her feel shouldn't. Its okay to settle in and get comfortable but don't allow your comfort ability to turn into complacency. If she's a treasure then rest assure you aren't the only one who sees and wants her. Don't let another man be willing to go further than you are to show appreciation for your woman. If she's a good girl, she'll bring her expectations to the forefront. But, if you're a real man you'll stay so consistent that she never has to.

As the relationship grows things naturally change but how you make her feel shouldn't.

Show Her Off

Make sure she knows you're proud of her. If you aren't proud of her then you shouldn't be with her. It's not about everyone being in your business, it's about making sure she knows her importance to you isn't a secret. Making it clear that you're in a relationship does not require you to share the details of your relationship. Be a man about it; don't use the same old excuses you've always used just to be slick. Allowing yourself to be seen in public doesn't kill strong relationships; it only exposes the weak ones. If she's a good woman and treats you right and you all have a good relationship then there's no reason not to be proud of her. You don't have to have her as your screen saver or post pictures of her all day, but it shouldn't be a surprise to people when they find out you're in a relationship. Men only hide things they're ashamed of. Don't make her feel like you're more proud of your shoes or your car than you are of her.

If she's a good woman and treats you right; and you all have a good relationship then there's no reason not to be proud of her.

Don't False Advertise

Don't be a tinfoil warrior but tell her you're a knight in shining armor. Most men let their mouths set a pace their feet can't keep up with. If she's communicating with you then she's interested. You don't have to sell her pipe dreams to get in good with her, just be yourself. A real woman will expect you to be all the man that you say you are. Don't let your words set you up for failure. If you're going to talk it then you also have to be prepared to walk it. One of the most cowardly things you can do as a man is try to make your woman feel crazy for holding you to a standard. A real woman expects certain things from a real man and if you're about avoiding expectations then you aren't ready for what a real woman has to offer. Don't sell dreams, don't fabricate the truth, and don't exaggerate what's real. Let the man you are and what you stand for represent you accurately and genuinely because the right woman will appreciate it.

Be Proactive

Don't be a "whatever" man. If you want to be respected then be an "I know exactly what I want" man. An indecisive man can quickly be taken for a weak man if he isn't careful. Don't allow yourself to be mistaken for something you are not. Know what you want, know how you want it, and know what you need to do to get it. Women respect men who can make a decision. When you're asking a woman on a date and it's in the early stages of developing a relationship, know where you want to take her and have a plan. Simple things like that let her know you were looking forward to spending time with her enough to plan and that you're man enough to put together a nice evening without her help. No woman wants a weak man. So if she feels like she can walk all over you then she won't want to walk with you.

When you're asking a woman on a date and it's in the early stages of developing a relationship, know where you want to take her and have a plan.

Be Encouraging

You should always encourage your woman. Push her to chase her dreams and to do new things. For most women, the most attractive thing you can do as a man is show her something she hasn't seen before. Don't stand in the background and say "good job." Actually be there and get engaged with what she's doing. If she's into something, you don't have to be in order to show her that you appreciate it. Support her in what she does and always encourage her to do more. If you're not willing to put energy towards trying to bring the best out of her then you shouldn't be with her. Women are naturally supportive when it comes to the man they care about. It is your responsibility to reciprocate that and show her how much you value what she does, especially when it isn't something she's doing for you.

If you're funny and carefree, then be funny and carefree, you don't have to be serious all the time just because the woman you like can't take a joke.

Don't Try To Be What You Think She Likes

Be yourself. There is nothing more annoying to a woman than a man "faking" it. If you are not authentically being "you," a real woman will spot it every single time. You don't have to fit any mold of what you think she likes. If she doesn't like you for who you are as a man, then that's just something you will have to accept. If you're a nice guy, don't change. There are enough women out there who will appreciate the "nice guy." Don't get disgruntled when people say nice guys finish last because that's what they save the best for. If you're funny and carefree, then be funny and carefree, you don't have to be serious all the time just because the woman you like can't take a joke. Date according to who you're genuinely compatible with, not according to whom you think you'll look good with. If you feel like you can't be yourself and impress a woman then you're trying to impress the wrong kind of women. A good woman will always appreciate a man true enough to himself to stay comfortably in his own lane.

49

Pay Attention To Her

You have to pick up on her tendencies and interest. A woman loves a man that "gets" her. Show her that you know the "real" her. Know her strengths well enough to make them stronger and learn her weaknesses in a way that allows you to make them better. There's a reason for the way she does certain things, care enough about her to figure out what that reason is. Most men miss their diamond in the rough because they're lazy. They expect their treasure to be on the grounds surface and it doesn't work like that. You have to pay attention to a woman in more ways than one in order to get to know her. If she's not worth investing extra time into then you have to let her go.

A woman loves a man that "gets" her.

Don't Be Unfair In Your Expectations

Only a good man can expect to reap the benefits of having a good woman. If you're a guy that plays games because you think all women are no good, then no good women is all those games will get you. Don't expect a woman to treat you like a King if you're treating her like a peasant. You can't expect to be trusted if you claim to have trust issues. Make sure your expectations are fair and reasonable. If you can't cook, then you have no room to complain about the lack of home cooked meals. If you aren't willing to reach the standard yourself, don't set it for your woman or anyone else. You can't expect somebody to appreciate your flaws if all you want to do is ridicule theirs. If you want to be taken as you are, be prepared to do the same for somebody else. Unfair expectations don't do anything but set you up for unwanted disappointments.

Chapter Seven

Reasons Why Most Relationships Fail

The unhealthiest of relationships are those that attempt to relate by playing games and using ineffective rules. A relationship isn't a battlefield for pride and if you treat it like one; you'll lose the war for real love. A successful relationship is not an anomaly but it's a reality. A successful relationship requires two people who want to be together enough to work things out.

For Single People Who Still Understand the Value of Relationships

Miscommunication

It is a certainty that when communication fails, assumptions succeed. There is nothing productive about arguing. Couples that argue do nothing but fight each other with pride. If yelling and screaming is the only way you can talk about things, you'll never get far when trying to work them out. Talk things out in an effective way and learn how to find a common ground to stand on. Being on the same page isn't always as important as understanding the two of you are in the same book. Sometimes you and your partner will see things differently but that doesn't mean it should lead to an argument. Learn how to discuss and talk things out in a way that brings the situation some resolve without using words you might regret.

Being on the same page isn't always as important as understanding the two of you are in the same book.

Lies

There is nothing worse than a person brave enough to do something but acts cowardly and lies about it when confronted. Honesty should never be a problem for a person who genuinely wants happiness. If you're lying to somebody trying to protect yourself, all you're really doing is playing yourself. Lies do nothing but create divides in relationships. There's no point in doing something today that you know you'll have to lie about later. The most disgusting thing you can be is a liar. Not only does it show a lack of concern for anyone else, it also shows you don't even respect your own word. If you want a healthy productive relationship then keep the lies out of it. You don't have to be perfect, just be true enough to stand by your mistakes. If it's really a mistake, you won't feel the need to lie about it.

Too Many Outside Influences

Don't pay attention to what your friends are doing in their relationships or lives. What works for them, won't always work for you. The only important voices in your relationship are those of you and your partner. Not your boss, not your mother, and certainly not your friends. Don't expect anybody else to work your problems out for you. If they didn't break it for you and your partner, they can't fix it for either of you. Be content and comfortable with going to each other for problems just as you do for pleasure. You don't need your friends in your business to tell you what's right or wrong. Write your problems down on paper and work through them together. The more people you welcome into your relationship, the harder it will be to keep it together.

Be content and comfortable with going to each other for problems just as you do for pleasure.

Pride

Most relationships fail because couples fight with pride more than they work with love. A man's pride will make him keep going thru a red light; a woman's insecurities will have her stopping at a green one. Don't fight to prove a point, fight to stay together. It shouldn't be a constant battle of who's right and who's wrong because successful relationships care more about preserving virtues than they do about stacking victories. Put your pride to the side so that your happiness can step to the forefront. It does a couple no good to be full of pride, especially when they claim to be in love. Don't get so caught up in fighting just to fight, that you forget what you're fighting for.

Bitterness About The Past

If you're carrying around unnecessary baggage, you're weighing down the progress of today. You have to let go of what happened in your previous relationships and trust that you've learned from them in ways that make you more equipped to love. If you can't let the problems of the past go, you'll be forced to watch the possibilities of the future fade. Don't let the bitterness of the past block you from bettering your future. Take the good that you've experienced in previous relationships and make it better. Take the bad that you've experienced in previous relationships and turn it into a learning lesson. It's all about growing from what you've experienced in a way that makes you more optimistic about future relationships, not pessimistic because of your limited past.

If you can't let the problems of the past go, you'll be forced to watch the possibilities of the future fade

Insecurities

If you're not confident in who you are and what you can bring to the table, you'll be stuck eating alone. Understand that your partner isn't perfect; don't allow your insecurities to manipulate their mistakes for malice. A key part of relationships is helping one another grow. You have to make sure that the insecurities don't turn into insufficiencies. If you know something bothers your partner then respect it and be mindful of what you might do to push that button. Don't manipulate your partner and try to use their concerns against them. Just because they don't want to tolerate certain things, doesn't always make them insecure. Respect their stance on whatever the issue is and if you feel strongly about it, find a place where you both can compromise.

Worrying

Don't worry about things you can't control. It's a poisonous habit and if you're not careful, you'll unknowingly allow it to kill your relationship. You can't control everything that happens and trying to will only limit your happiness. If you waste too much time worrying, it will stop you from embracing things you were meant to enjoy. No one likes uncertainty but if you have faith, you understand what's meant to happen will always happen the way it's supposed to. If you feel like the person you're with is truly meant for you, then you won't waste time playing games to make them stay. Accept that God's plan for your life is far greater than anything that you could ever come up with for yourself. God values and wants the best for you. Stop trusting your heart to minions and give it to the master.

You can't control everything that happens and trying to will only limit your happiness.

A Lack Of Direction

If you don't know where you're going in your personal life, there's no way you will be able to guide a relationship to anywhere resembling "happily ever after." Understand where you are enough to know if you're even in the position to relate to a relationship. If you have to ask yourself if you're ready for a relationship, then you're probably not. Let God lead you to where HE wants you to be. Along God's path for you, you'll find the relationship that is meant for you. Having direction helps you understand devotion. When you know where you're going, you can confidently lead a healthy relationship. When you're trying to do things the right way, don't skip steps. You must be honest enough with yourself to be patient and allow things to happen naturally.

Unclear and Unrealistic Expectations

Men, handle your own business. Don't expect your partner to do everything for you as if she was your mother. Ladies, don't expect your boyfriend to be a perfect man, just as you make mistakes, he will too. Understand that having an expectation sets a standard for the person setting it and the person being asked to live up to it. You can't expect a loyal woman if you're an inconsistent man. You can't expect a complete man if you're an incomplete woman. You have to make sure your expectations match your existence. If you want a superman then make sure you're a wonder woman. You have to make what you're expecting clear to the person you're expecting it from. No one is looking for perfection when it comes to relationships but everyone looks for something real and there's nothing wrong with expecting to get it.

...what you build together grows stronger

Unhealthy Dating Process

Most relationships breakdown when rough times hit because they are built on unstable ground. The courting process lays a firm foundation for what will be built in the relationship. Timing is everything so don't cheat yourself by trying to take shortcuts to happiness. When you allow time and experience to bring you closer; then what you build together grows stronger. You can't get blindsided by infatuation. Make sure they can consistently show you greatness, not just glimpses of goodness. When things are going well, people tend to start rushing and that's why most relationships turn out bad. Take your time and get to know more about the person than their favorite color. We all understand fun and happiness, but get to know how they respond to pain and if they're built to handle rough times. Date with honesty and genuine truth, don't hold back just because of your past. A healthy dating process will produce a healthy lasting relationship.

Chapter Eight

Ingredients Of True Love

The most undervalued part of love is the unconditional part. It's the part of love that allows you to have an orange, your partner to have an apple, but you both agree that it's fruit. Unconditional love is the part of love that understands differences. True love isn't a myth or some dream to be sold; it's real, and its ingredients are found when you have two people willing to do whatever is required to have it.

For Single People Who Still Understand the Value of Relationships

Compassion

It is important that you know how to get through to your partner. Regardless of whether you're pissed off or disappointed, always remember that the value of your relationship is more important than the issues in the argument. Work with each other, not against each other. You have to be able to look past the anger and see their heart. Understand that if you're choosing to love, then you're choosing to care, and you have to care all the time, not just when you're happy. Compassion eases things; it bridges the gaps that pride and fear create. Regardless of the mistakes you or your partner make, it's necessary to maintain a degree of compassion. See past what's on the surface and try to understand where they are coming from and what they may have been thinking.

Love is the ultimate responsibility

Responsibility

Love is the ultimate responsibility. It requires you to think about more than yourself and to act with consideration for others. When you choose love, you become the guardian of a heart and you're responsible for protecting it as you would your own. When your partner is down, it's your responsibility to bring them up. When your love is hurting, it's your responsibility to help them find healing. When your friend is lost, it's your responsibility to help them get direction. Love doesn't drop the ball when it comes, love comes through in the clutch; love is always there when it counts. Love is more than the result of a bunch of feelings for a person; love is an acceptance of responsibility to a heart. You have to look at the person you care about and accept that it is your responsibility to be there through the ups and the downs.

Patience

If you don't think it's something worth being patient for then it's not something you will value having. When you know it's worth the wait, patience will never be a problem. Love is never in a hurry. Love is never in a rush. Love never moves in haste. The only people who rush love are the ones who don't trust it. Don't be one of those people who move so fast that the only way you can stop is to crash. Take your time and allow things to develop into everything that they can be. If it's real, there's no need to rush it because it will happen the way it's supposed to. Always respect the virtue of patience. Love understands and respects the fact that timing is everything. Patience is the key to securing and preserving God's promises.

Love is never in a rush.

Passion

Passion is the ultimate gateway to true love in relationships. It's that ineffable adoration that two lovers share for one another. Passion knows no obstacles; it does whatever, whenever and wherever in order to thrive. When two people are truly passionate about one another, it's evident and it draws them nearer. Passionate love is the most fulfilling love because it connects people in a way that words can't describe. Passion in love is so vital because it keeps the love fluid, warm, and exciting. When you can look at your partner and see the fire in their eyes burning for you, it compels you to love a little harder, to try a little more, and to do a little better.

Trust

You can have love for somebody you don't trust but it is impossible to be in love with somebody you don't trust. If a person has problems trusting they will have problems loving. If they cannot trust then they should not be trusted. Trust is sacred when it comes to true love. You have to maintain the trust between you and your partner because it affects all areas of the relationship. A lack in trust affects communication, it alters perception, and it limits the progress of love. Value trust and do whatever you can to keep it so that the love you share isn't limited. Love cannot flourish in the absence of trust. Without trust, most lovers are ruled by fear. Trust that your partner will make good decisions, trust that your lover has good intentions, and trust that your friend will be there when they say they will.

...love is lost as a result of dead desires.

Desire

Desire is the ingredient that gives your love a unique flavor. It is important to remain in a state physically, mentally, and spiritually that renders you desirable. Most love is lost as a result of dead desires. It happens when you change in such a way that stops giving the person something to long for. Don't underestimate the power of desires. All forms of cheating have some form of desire in common. Whether it's the desire for intimate conversation, the desire for peace of mind, or the desire to have attention, make sure you understand and know what desires your lover has so that you are able to meet and satisfy them. If you're in love with a good person, everything you are will be what they desire and if they want more, they'll teach you how to be that.

Clarity

Love is always more focused on the bigger picture than it is with the minor problems. Love has no intent to hurt or bring pain; it realizes that imperfections in people don't change God's perfection in love. Love in its purest form isn't spiteful, deceptive, or vengeful. If somebody hides something from you, it's not out of love. If somebody lies to you, it's not to protect you in the name of love. What most people fail to realize is that love honors genuine intentions. Love has direction and it is guided by whatever vision you've set for it. If things start to get cloudy in your love life, it's because you haven't actively tried to maintain its clarity. You can't cloud love with frustrations, doubts, and fears about things that are beyond your control. The best way to keep clarity is to let what's important stay important and to let the irrelevant things go.

Love has no intent to hurt or bring pain.

Hope

Love is optimism. Love understands that hurt people hurt people but it has hope that if given the chance, healed people can heal people. Love understands that things don't always happen how we want them to but love still has hope for the best of possibilities. Love see's the reality of certain situations but it still maintains hope that thing can get better. Don't ever let circumstance or pain steal the hope that you have in love. If you're a good person and you have faith, you should have hope as well. Hope believes in more than what's in front of you. Hope is seeing past the arguments and knowing that things get better. Hope is accepting the disappointments but acknowledging that you have the strength to keep going. Love is hope.

Perseverance

Lovers and quitters have never had anything in common. If you think anything about love is easy, you're setting yourself up for major disappointments. Successful love takes work and it takes two people who are committed to working things out in the midst of whatever challenges may come their way. Real love will endure and persevere regardless of circumstance. Love does not understand quitting; it can't comprehend walking out just because things are bad. Love perseveres and love works things out. If the relationship you're in makes you want to quit when things get rough and makes you want to run every time you get a little scared, then you're not in love. But when you're relationship makes you want to fight when things get a little rocky and unites you with your partner when the test comes, then you're in love because real love perseveres.

Love does not understand quitting; it can't comprehend walking out just because things are bad.

Loyalty

Love does not change; it is sovereign. Regardless of whether things are up or down, love still stands firm. Love is loyal; it's not a fair weather thing. It doesn't matter whether it's sunny or raining, love doesn't leave; it stands by you. Don't get swayed by the pessimist and the people who only believe in loving during the good times and leaving when the bad times come. Love is about sticking it out through anything. Loyalty and love go hand in hand but always be mindful not to be manipulated by people who claim to love you but aren't loyal to you. There's a fine line between loyalty and stupidity and real love will never have you on the wrong side of that.

Other Titles
by Rob Hill Sr.

*I GOT YOU

*ABOUT SOMETHING REAL

TRUCE
Healing Your Heart After Disappointment

*THE MISSING PIECE
(COMING SPRING/SUMMER 2018)

Website: robhillsr.com
Instagram: robhillsr
Twitter: @RobHillSr
Facebook: RobHillSr
SoundCloud:
https://soundcloud.com/robhillsr
YouTube:
https://www.youtube.com/user/RobHillSr